Picture Framing for Beginners

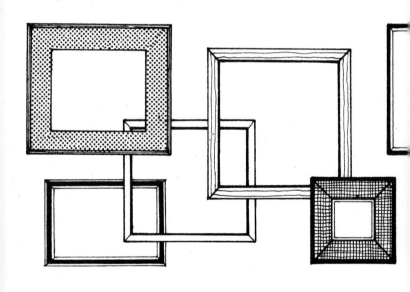

Picture Framing for Beginners

Prudence Nuttall

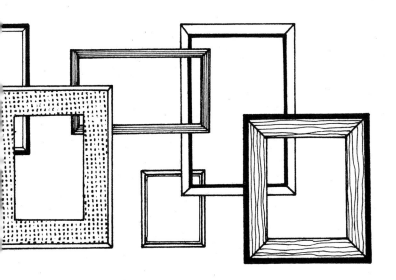

Studio Vista London

Watson-Guptill Publications New York

Acknowledgement

With special thanks to John Eriksen who took the photographs appearing in this book.

General Editors Brenda Herbert and Janey O'Riordan
© Prudence Nuttall 1968
Reprinted 1970
Published in London by Studio Vista Limited
Blue Star House, Highgate Hill, London N19
and in New York by Watson-Guptill Publications
165 West 46th Street, New York 10036
Library of Congress Catalog Card Number 68–16176
Set in 9 on 11 pt Univers
Printed Offset Litho and bound in Great Britain by
Cox & Wyman Ltd, London, Fakenham and Reading
UKSBN 289.36922.3

Contents

Introduction

Picture framing is a craft which has been in existence for hundreds of years, and it is primarily concerned with the protection and the preservation of pictures. Methods and fashions have changed, but some of the processes have remained. Many of the mouldings still used today are of a traditional pattern, and some, in fact, are even named after the artists who designed them specially to suit their own particular work. An example of this is the black and gilt moulding known as Hogarth, which is still one of the standard types of moulding used extensively for engravings, prints and maps.

Professional picture framing is a small world of proficient craftsmen, some of whom produce a high standard of specialized work such as gilding. Except in a few isolated cases, it is not generally possible to learn the trade apart from being apprenticed to a picture framer. This has lead to a lack of general knowledge about framing, and, consequently, there is somewhat of a mystery attached to it. But no special skills are required to start making simple frames apart from an ability to use tools and an aptitude for precise work involving a certain degree of patience. An interest in creative work and an appreciation of the materials you are working with will help to give an understanding of what will enhance the picture and show it off to the best advantage.

With the general increase of interest in paintings since the end of the war, many people find pleasure in producing their own pictures as well as looking at those of other people. Considerable satisfaction can be gained from this as well as a knowledge of the use of paint and different techniques. However, framing pictures can provide some difficulties, usually of expense, as an amateur may not feel it is worthwhile to spend much money on a frame. But, if you wish to exhibit your work, you will almost certainly be required to have it framed.

This book has been written to try and help you make simple frames for yourself, as well as to give you some idea of what is possible, should you want your paintings framed professionally.

Most people can recognize whether or not a picture has been well framed, but unless they have had some experience, it is not always easy to know why. The variety of treatments can be confusing and, as the result can make a great difference to the whole appearance of the picture, it is as well to have some general idea of what you are aiming at before you set out to do it yourself.

For anyone who is considering making his own frames, it is an excellent idea to visit galleries and museums and be generally aware of pictures in other people's houses so that you notice how the types of work have been framed. After a while you will have some idea of what seem to be the most successful results.

Fig. 1 *Bonnard print.* Small black and white print framed simply with mount (mat)

1 Choosing a frame

Choosing a frame depends to some extent on personal preference, although such factors as the colour, proportion and texture of both the frame and the picture in relation to each other should all be taken into account. On the whole avoid over-framing and gimmicky frames, as the frame should not attract attention from the picture. At the beginning, stick to simple mouldings — with these and a few essential tools, adequate frames can be made. Once your confidence has increased, you will be ready to try something more complicated, such as building up complex frames from different mouldings.

Basically, every frame should be chosen to suit the picture rather than the room in which it is going to hang, although, as there are different ways of framing the same picture satisfactorily, some variety is possible to suit the setting. For example, in a traditional room with antique furniture, it is better to stick to a conventional moulding, say a black and gilt Hogarth, or waxed wood for prints, or a dull gold for an oil painting. In a more modern room angular mouldings, or frames in a sharp white or metallic silver can look very effective, whereas they might look a bit stark in another setting. A heavy frame can be used on a small picture if it is to hang in a prominent position in the room.

Some people prefer to dispense with frames and mount pictures on blockboard (hardboard or Masonite), flush with the edges, so that they hang slightly away from the wall. This method affords no protection to the picture, and is only satisfactory for works of little value. There is also a system of fixing adjustable wireclips to the picture with glass and a hardboard backing. Though this is not strictly picture framing, it is a useful way of displaying something of temporary interest, such as a poster or sketch, the advantage being that when the interest has passed, the same fittings can then be used for something else.

With actual framing, there are two general categories, frames with glass, and frames without. Glass is required on anything needing protection from dust which cannot be cleaned. Drawings, watercolours, engravings, documents, pastels, gouaches and etchings and anything that requires a mount quickly deteriorate without some sort of protection. Large works such as brass rubbings or maps on the other hand are too impractical and costly to frame under glass owing to the area involved quite apart from the resulting weight. These, however, can be protected by several thin applications of watercolour spray varnish. (Note that the paper for brass rubbings is generally fragile, and should be treated with particular care.) Reproduction prints can also be varnished (see chapter 3).

Pictures in oils or acrylic paint do not generally need the protection of glass as they can be varnished, though glass may be preferred on a small painting if the colour is pale or the work particularly delicate. Most drawings and prints, with the exception of those with wide borders and those that are particularly large, are improved by the use of a mount to give suitable 'breathing space' to the picture. Proportions and colours for mounts are referred to in chapter 3. Bold drawings or reproductions of oil paintings can be treated as oils and framed without mounts, in a heavier moulding. But mounted work should on the whole have a simple frame. Waxed wood or narrow gold or silver half-round prepared mouldings are often the most successful. Colours suitable for finishing a plain wood section are referred to in chapter 5.

Framing oils

This is a question of protecting the canvas as well as displaying the picture. Modern oils, particularly large abstracts, often look best in a very narrow baguette frame or even just a length of wood stripping paper round the edge to cover the nail heads of the canvas. This has the advantage of obscuring none of the composition if the painting reaches right to the edge of the canvas.

Generally, however, a heavier moulding, of up to 2" wide would be most suitable for an average 24" x 20" canvas, wider for a larger canvas. Varieties of mouldings depend on what is

Fig. 2 Virgilio Guzzi *Portrait 1944*. Oil painting in 3″ prepared moulding

available, but interesting combinations of narrow mouldings can be built up to form a wider section. If the moulding is natural wood it can be coloured as in chapter 5. Other excellent frames for oil paintings can be made by using mouldings already prepared with gilt. Gilt mouldings are obtainable in an antiqued, dull finish— suitable for a dark, rather heavy painting, or in a brighter gilt for a painting that is lighter or more brilliant in tone. A slip (insert), or inner frame, next to the surface of the picture is advisable with oils. The visual effect is better as it softens the hard edge between the frame and the picture. It can be covered in a neutral linen or coloured to suit the picture (chapter 5). The width of this slip (insert) depends on the overall proportions. For example, a wide scoop or slope opens out the picture requiring only a narrow frame, whereas a heavier moulding (2" to 3" wide) is better with a narrow slip (insert) of about 1" (fig. 7). In either case always avoid having the frame and slip of equal width.

You may feel that a gold leaf frame would really suit the picture best, but gilding is difficult to do yourself without proper training. It is a craft which takes years of experience to perfect because of the several elaborate processes involved. I have included a short section on it, but I would stress that if you are particularly anxious to have a frame in gold leaf, it may ultimately be cheaper and easier to have it made by a professional framemaker who specializes in gilding. Unlike the rather metallic look of gilt, gold gives a warm brightness, owing to the red and yellow in the initial underlay which softens any hard appearance. Silver leaf can also be obtained, but this is even harder to lay than gold and does not really fall within the scope of this book.

Framing need not necessarily be limited only to pictures. Mirrors, fabric collage, tapestries are just a few of the examples. The possibilities are endless: any small object, which you want to preserve and display can be fitted into a box frame; low relief carvings, miniatures, cameos, seals, coins, even unusual pebbles look most attractive if well mounted on a suitable coloured background.

2 Tools and equipment

If you already have a workbench and the usual tools to be found in any handyman's house, then you will not need to buy many new tools to start framing. Although a professional frame-maker has some very expensive equipment, cheaper versions are available which will be quite sufficient to produce respectable frames.

When buying tools it is well to remember that cheap ones are not always efficient; it is better to pay a bit more and buy something which is going to last and do the job well, and as the basic tools are not expensive the difference is well worth paying.

Space is usually limited for most people, so that bulk buying of mouldings and boards is often out of the question. Some manufacturers however, will only supply these in quantity, and obviously it is more economical not to deal in small amounts. A frame-maker for instance has to stock a wide variety of mouldings to deal with all the different types of work which are brought in, and to avoid delay in delivery from the suppliers. But as you will probably have some specific work in mind to start with, say a collection of prints or a few of your own paintings, you will find that you will have adequate space as you will be working with only one or two mouldings at a time.

The bench where you are going to work is the first consideration. It may, if you are lucky, be a proper workbench or if not, the kitchen table will do. You cannot always have ideal working conditions, and as this is a book on simple frame-making it would be discouraging to insist upon them. The main idea is that you make the most of what you have.

Whatever work table you use, make sure that it is absolutely steady on the floor, as it is impossible to do anything if the working surface rocks unsteadily beneath you. It is also a help if you can walk round it, certainly round three sides, for if you are working on a large frame it will probably extend over the edge of the table. To avoid undue backache the ideal height for the average person is about 3' 0" – working on lower levels can slow down the work and be very tiring. The surface of the table must be level, if it is not, a sheet of heavy hardboard or plywood cut to the same size is the answer. It will also help protect the surface from any cuts or stains.

Within easy reach of the workbench there should be some undisturbed space where frames can be left to dry without fear of being jarred before the glue has set. The corners are vulnerable when first joined, and take about 2–3 hours to dry in a warm temperature before the work can proceed. If you haven't the space to lay them flat, they can hang on one side – not of course by the corner – from a peg on the wall. This also applies to the finishing of frames if they are being stained or painted, which you can read more about in chapter 5. But here we are concerned with having sufficient space, and the correct temperature for the purposes of drying. A damp atmosphere will hinder the drying process, but the use of an electric fan heater will help considerably, if you are in a hurry.

It is easier to concentrate on one process at a time, i.e. mounting, woodwork or finishing, as you can then organise one set of equipment and just have round you what is needed for the particular job. The average kitchen table cannot accommodate sheets of mounting card, paste pots, paper etc., as well as newly-made frames and the various pots of paint and tins of stain needed for finishing.

If possible, have a large drawer for keeping the pictures flat after you have mounted them where they can stay undisturbed while the frame is being made. It is, of course, important not to get any marks or dirt on them before the glass is fitted. The same drawer can be used for storing sheets of tinted paper to cover mounts, as it is essential that they also be kept clean and flat. Creases are not always easy to remove afterwards. Boards for laying pictures on, and the mounting boards themselves can be stacked upright, preferably behind a piece of furniture if they are large to avoid the corners being knocked. Oil paintings, which are very vulnerable, must be stored in a dry place, but away from direct heat or radiators, and where there are no sharp edges to pierce through the canvas.

Finally, good lighting is essential so that you can really see what you are doing.

Tools for woodwork

The most important piece of special equipment is a mitre-box to cut the corners at an angle of 45° accurately. The ultimate success of a frame depends on this, because if the corners are not correct, the whole frame will be uneven. Therefore, accuracy is essential. This could be your biggest outlay, for the better the mitre-box the easier it is to get a professional look with a limited amount of experience. Mitre-boxes vary in price considerably.

I would suggest that the best compromise is a box which is capable of cutting mouldings up to 2" wide by 1¾" deep. It is fitted with adjustable depth stops and should be used with a 12" back or tennon saw (fig. 4a).

Beechwood mitre-boxes (fig. 3) are simple boxes without ends, with 4 slots cut into them at angles of 45° so that the moulding can be laid in the box, and the saw fitted into the slots to cut through the moulding at the same angle. These are best used with small, light mouldings, although they are designed to take one up to 4" wide. The disadvantage of this type of box is that unless the saw is kept absolutely vertical during the cutting, it tends to eat away the sides of the slot, which then gradually becomes looser and the mitres consequently less accurate. A slightly more expensive version has adjustable saw-guides with metal reinforcements at the top of the slots. The guide screws are

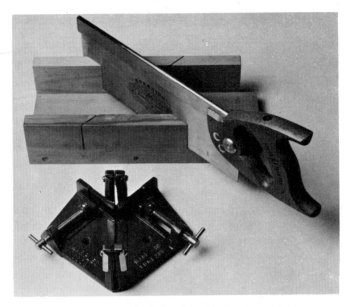

Fig. 3 Beechwood mitre-box and mitre-cutter

slackened so that the saw slides freely but at the same time remains vertical. The 12″ tenon saw is recommended for both these mitre-boxes.

In the higher price range are precision mitre-boxes which are supplied with a saw blade and have a recessed surface to the base to avoid damaging the saw teeth. The prices of these vary considerably according to whether the model cuts up to a width and depth of 2″ or cuts up to a width of $6\frac{1}{4}$″ and a depth of $4\frac{3}{4}$″. These have frame saws which are lighter in weight and more accurate than tenon saws, since their properly tightened blades do not deviate so easily. Setting is possible to any required angle by means of a swivel. There is also a length stop which can be attached to either front side of the mitre-box, and which is used for cutting off a number of workpieces of the same length without repeated measuring.

Although this type of box is naturally more efficient, it would only be an economical buy if you intend to make a large quantity of frames, so to start with it is advisable to choose the cheaper sort and see how you get on.

Various grades of sandpaper are used for finishing. Grade 2 is most useful, but in cases where the wood has to be very smooth –if the moulding is to be left plain and waxed, or coloured for instance–a finer grade is needed. A cork rubber is useful as a sanding block.

Wet and dry abrasive paper. For sharpening the blade of the mountcutting (mat) knife. This is used with a little water, but never oil, which could leave ineradicable stains on the paper.

a *Tenon saw*
12" for using with mitre-boxes,
sawing hardboard, and
general purposes

b *Rule*
3' 0" folding carpenters' rule
measured in $\frac{1}{8}$" and $\frac{1}{16}$".
Must be accurate

c *Blockplane*
For planing rough edges of
mouldings at the back of the
frame and bevelling off sharp
corners

d *Trysquare*
This is useful when testing the
angles of the frame to ensure a
correct angle of 45°.

e, f *Screwdrivers*
Larger for general purposes,
smaller used in fitting work, for
fixing mirror plates, spring clips etc.

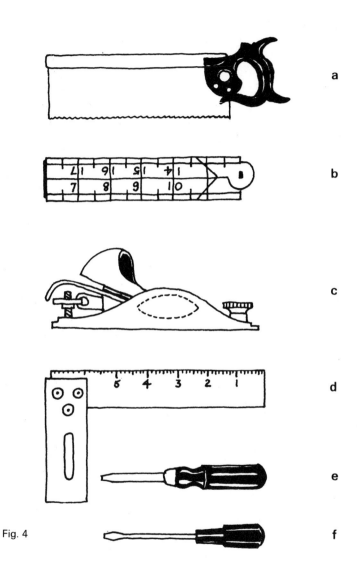

Fig. 4

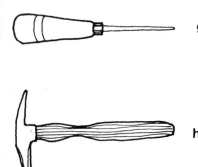

g Bradawl (awl)

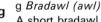

g *Bradawl (awl)*
A short bradawl (awl) is useful for starting holes in mitred corners before hammering in nails. It is also used in fitting pictures when putting in screw-eyes for hanging. A hand or electric drill is better for heavier mouldings, but on smaller ones a bradawl (awl) is sufficient

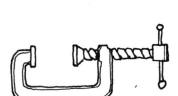

h

h *Hammer*
Best for general use is a light pattern-maker's (tack) hammer. This is used both for joinery work and fitting

i

i *G cramps (C clamps)*
Most useful size 4" to 6"

j *Pincers (pliers)*
For removing nails and unfitting pictures

j

k *Nailset*
This is for driving nails below the surface when joining the mitred corners, so that the holes can afterwards be filled and the surface smoothed off. Nails for joining have small rounded heads.

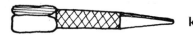

k

Tools and equipment for mounting and laying

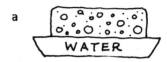

a *Cellulose sponge and water*
For damping certain papers prior to laying

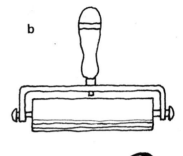

b *Decorator's felt paint roller*
Not less than 6" long for rolling out papers when laying down

c *General purpose large scissors*
For cutting paper, fabrics etc

d *2" paste brush*
This must always be cleaned after use, and kept free of any particles of dried paste. If these should adhere to the underneath of the paper which is being laid, they will show through as little bumps

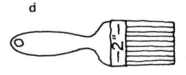

e *Mountcutter's knife (mat knife)*
The blade, which is pushed through the body of the knife can be screwed into position. It should be ground to a fine flat point as shown, and must be kept very sharp at all times. After the initial grinding on a water stone it can be kept

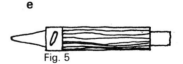

Fig. 5

sharp by rubbing on fine abrasive paper, used with a little water. On no account must oil be used, as this may leave marks on the paper which cannot be removed

f *Trimming (X-acto) knife with replaceable blades*
This is used for cutting card and linens, and trimming the brown (backing) paper used for stripping the backs of the finished frames. Again, always work with a sharp blade and discard any blunt ones as they will tear the paper. Razor blades can be used, but they are harder to control

g *Thin sheet diamond cutter for glass*
(In USA the Red Devil glass cutter is easily available for this purpose).
This tool actually cuts the glass whereas the ordinary

glass cutter—(h)—merely scores it, and does not give such satisfactory results, as the glass is inclined to shatter

i *Upholsterers' pincers (pliers)*
These are not essential, but are useful for stretching

canvasses tightly over a
stretcher

j *45° straight-edged perspex
(Plexiglas) set-square
(45° triangle)*
For measuring mounts (mats)
accurately

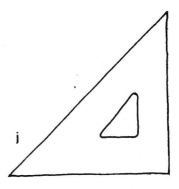

j

k *Engineers' metal straight-edge*
For marking out mounts (mats)
and cutting strips of material
for panels. Cut along the
non-bevelled edge, as the
knife is likely to slip under
the bevel.

k

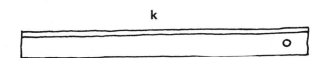

Boards and paper

Ticket board
This is used for laying (wet mounting). The board comes already faced on one side, so that it doesn't warp when the other side is pasted. Any board can be used as long as it has a flat surface, but if warping should occur, line the back with ordinary brown paper.

Mounting (matting) board
This is faced off on both sides and comes in various sizes. It can be white or tinted, and is available in different thicknesses which are referred to as sheets (or ply). 6 sheet (or ply) is generally used, but 8 sheet (or ply) will give a cleaner, deeper bevel. 12 sheet can be effective to show up a very small picture, but it is harder to cut. It must be smooth and free from marks and flaws.

Mount (mat) paper
Different papers can be used to surface the mounting (matting) boards before the window is cut. There are a wide variety of papers suitable for this purpose, such as the handmade Japanese papers which come in beautiful, subtle colours, Ingres paper, textured papers, silk wallpaper, marbled papers, and so on. Sizes vary considerably so be careful that the paper you choose is available in a size large enough for the mount (mat) you require to make.

Tissue paper
Acid free tissue paper is helpful to protect already mounted (matted) work while the frame is being made. It is also used when pressing out work during laying (wet mounting), being placed between the roller and the picture.

Newspapers
It is advisable to have quite a quantity of old newspapers handy when mounting (matting) and laying (mounting), and preferably those with larger pages. Discard any paper as soon as it has paste or water on it, since it is essential to work as cleanly as possible if the mounts (mats) are not to become marked.

Stripping paper (paper tape)
2" gummed brown paper is used to seal the edges of the backs of the frames, after the hardboard has been nailed into place. This is to prevent dust getting into the frame later on.

Other materials

Book cloth linen
This is a finely textured stiff cloth which can be used for covering mounts (mats), and slips (inserts) or inner frames for oil paintings. It comes in a variety of colours, and the reverse side can also be used if a paler shade of the same colour is needed.
Plain linen
Used as above for mounts (mats) and slips (inserts). As well as the suppliers listed at the end of the book, most large stores will have suitable linens of medium weight in their furnishing or dressmaking departments. Avoid any kind of synthetic material, as it is impossible to stick down successfully owing to the different chemical properties of both material and paste. Textures of linens vary, and a coarse texture should only be used when the picture is bold. (The linen should be used with the main weave going across from side to side, rather than top to bottom – (c.f. mounts).
Velvets
Ordinary cotton-backed furnishing velvet is good for backing small objects such as plaques and medals which can be set into the velvet. It is not successful for mounts as the glass flattens the pile, unless in a deep frame so that the glass is raised above it. Be careful to first hold the velvet up to the light to discover the direction of the pile – the darkest tone will give you a way to the direction in which it should run. Again, avoid synthetic velvet – the pile is too shiny apart from the difficulties of handling and laying down.
Silk
This needs great care in application, but can be used to good

effect on such work as delicate Japanese or Indian paintings. It should not be pasted on the surface of the board as the paste will mark the silk, but sewn from behind (fig. 28).

These are the most useful materials, but you can, of course, experiment with others as you gain experience.

Adhesives

Two adhesives are needed for general use which should cover most requirements.
a *A synthetic resin glue*
This is very strong and remains unaffected by changes in temperature. It dries quickly, particularly on porous surfaces. It is used for sticking wood to wood— mainly for joining the mitres of the frame. It can be obtained with a narrow applicator spout for easy control when working.

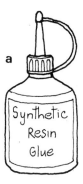

Fig. 6

b *A good starch-based paste*
This should, if necessary, be mixed with a little water to form a creamy consistency that will spread easily. It is relatively slow-drying to allow time for adjustments to be made, and is most effective when applied sparingly with a brush. It is intended primarily for light work such as laying down (wet mounting) pictures, covering mounting boards with paper and fabric and covering wooden panels with fabric. Rubber adhesives are not recommended for sticking paper as they may eventually discolour and show through the paper.

3 Preparing the work for framing

If the picture is to be mounted, this is the first stage of framing. And it is an important stage, since the mount, which is next to the picture, will be noticed before the frame, and this should therefore be chosen before the frame is made.

The selection of colours, materials and proportions all have to be considered; all are to some extent a question of personal taste, but to all of them certain general rules can be applied. The proportion of a mount should never compete with the proportions of the picture, and in fact one can generally assume that the smaller the picture the larger the relative of the mount. A small picture will look insignificant if it is framed close without a mount, and is much improved by either a wide mount or a heavy frame (fig. 7).

A medium sized print or drawing of say 16″ × 12″ will look best with a mount that has 2″ × 2½″ margins: that is to say the top and sides will be 2″ wide and the bottom 2½″ (fig. 8).

Fig. 7 Small picture showing different treatments

Fig. 8 Jean Easter *Cows*. Charcoal drawing with dark grey mount and simple wood frame

As a rule, the bottom margins looks narrower than the others and so needs to be made wider, though horizontal pictures are sometimes better with equal margins. If the print is larger it may need margins of $3'' - 3\frac{1}{2}''$, but for a very large work a mount will probably be unnecessary. For a picture which has a lot of white in it, a narrow mount may be sufficient or unnecessary (fig. 9). With practice, the eye will be able to judge what 'breathing space' is needed to avoid the picture looking cramped.

Although the colour of the mount is a matter of personal preference, there are certain basic rules which will limit the choice, and therefore make it easier. The colour of the mount should not compete with the picture, but rather be used to highlight it (fig. 48). If you have a very bright picture, keep the mount neutral. Bear in mind the difference between cool and warm

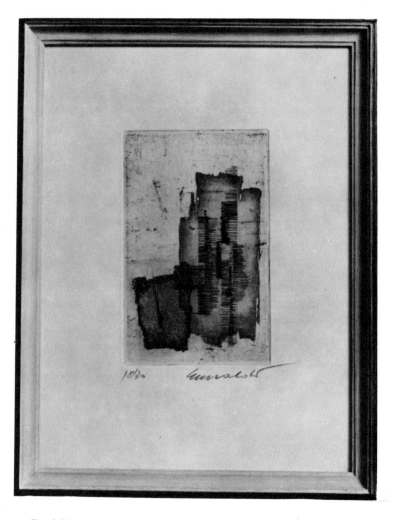

Fig. 9 Esmeraldo *Brown*. Etching in natural wood frame without a mount (mat)

colours. A picture in which blues and greens are predominant will be set off well by a warm beige, whereas with a hot red or orange, a cool grey or white would be better. Most watercolours look best with a cool mount, such as a blue-grey or green-grey. Etchings and drawings, having little or no colour in themselves can benefit from a tinted mount, but strong coloured mounts are best kept for prints where the decorative effect is the main consideration, such as reproductions of flower or bird prints, topographical subjects, playbills, black and white prints or photographs often look very effective treated in this way.

It is a good idea to have various scraps of different papers and boards on hand to put against the picture to see what the effect will be.

Laying (wet mounting)

Otherwise called wet-mounting means pasting the picture on to cardboard before making the mount (mat). This is not done in every case, as once a picture is laid it loses its value, so use your discretion, and if you are framing a picture for somebody else, get their permission first.

Prints with a plate mark or numbered lithographs should not be laid as they lose their value (fig. 9) — nor should these be trimmed to fit a frame; if extending over the edge of the mount, the surplus paper can be folded back. Unfixed pastels can only be laid (mounted) if great care is taken, as they smudge very easily when handled. Pictures on very thin or porous paper are also better left. But ordinary prints, sketches, small photographs, posters and maps are better laid (mounted) as it helps to keep them flat and free of creases. Large photographs are somewhat of a problem to lay (mount), as the paper can stretch unevenly and the photographic surface — particularly gloss surfaces — become unmanageably sticky very quickly. Moreover, if they are not exactly the right dampness when laid, blisters and folds will appear which cannot afterwards be removed. It would probably be better to have them dry mounted by a local photographer should they need any extra rigidity before framing.

When laying (mounting), it must be remembered that all papers have variable properties and will therefore react to water and paste in different ways. Whether you are laying (mounting) a picture down or covering a board with special paper to make a mount (mat), test a corner of the paper first. If it discolours or soaks up the water like blotting paper don't damp it, but paste the board and apply the paper directly to it. Most handmade or very fine papers are best treated in this way, but ordinary cartridge (drawing) or the paper normally used for reproductions should be damped before pasting.

Before you start work, first cover the working surface with several large sheets of clean newspaper, and have a sponge and bowl of clean water (fig. 10). Cut a piece of ticket board (a very thin cardboard) slightly larger than the paper you want to lay (mount) as it can be trimmed afterwards, and lay the paper face downwards. Most papers have a right and wrong side, so if you are covering a board for a mount (mat) make sure that the smoothest side will appear face up. Pass a damp sponge over the back, working with long even strokes (note that the sponge should not be too wet) (figs. 11-12). The paper should be made pliable enough to make the pasting down easy, and should be left for a few minutes to allow the water to penetrate right the way through. Several sheets can be damped at the same time, working on a fresh piece of newspaper for each, so that by the time you have finished the last one the first is ready for pasting. Have ready a small bowl of paste mixed with water to a consistency of thin smooth custard, free from any lumps or dried particles of old paste. Working with the same even strokes, brush the paste outwards from the middle of the picture. Make sure that all the edges and specially the corners are covered, and also that the paste is evenly distributed with no thick patches, as these will be difficult to press out later (fig. 13). Lift the picture up by the edges, lay it

Fig. 10 Preparing to lay (mount) watercolour by John Ward

lightly on the board (fig. 14), cover with a sheet of tissue paper and smooth out—first by hand to feel any unevenness, and then with the roller to smooth out any creases (fig. 15). Wipe off any surplus paste that has squeezed out under the edge of the picture with a dryish sponge. The laid picture should be kept flat when drying and preferably under pressure. To do this, first cover the picture with a sheet of tissue paper, then place over it a large piece of hardboard, and finally weigh it down with a heavy object.

If you do not wish to use glass on a reproduction print, the surface can be protected by varnish after it has been laid (mount-

Fig. 11

Fig. 12

Fig. 13

Figs 11-12 Damping the back of the watercolour

Fig. 13 Pasting the back of the watercolour

ed). But first you must give it two coats of weak size, otherwise the paper will absorb varnish unevenly. Size is made by dissolving a thin sheet of gelatine in boiling water (see p. 70), and it should be applied with a wide brush. Light varnish in an aerosol spray suitable for this purpose can easily be obtained from any artist's suppliers. Stand the picture upright and spray lightly all over from side to side. Several thin coats are better than one heavy one, for the varnish tends to become patchy or form dribbles (or curtains) if it is put on too thickly. It should be left to dry in a

Fig. 14 Laying (wet mounting) the watercolour on the ticket board

warm dust free atmosphere. Photographs can be protected with a light polishing of ordinary household white wax or bees' wax.

Embroideries and other fabric pictures should not on the whole be laid (mounted), though a close-textured material such as felt will take paste quite satisfactorily. A good way of making embroideries or small tapestries rigid before framing them is to cut a piece of card (cardboard) to the exact size of the area to be displayed, fold the edges of the material over this and secure it by pinning through the cut edges of the board with ordinary dressmaker's pins (fig. 16). This enables you to get the weave

Fig. 15 Rolling out watercolour protected by tissue paper

quite straight, by adjusting any unevenness as you go along.

Pictures that are not laid down (mounted), may be fixed to a board before being mounted (matted). Small works can be fixed with hinges cut from the brown gummed paper which is used in stripping the backs of the pictures. For anything larger, masking tape is safe to use as it can always be removed later without causing any damage. But avoid scotch tape or rubber adhesive as they not only tend to discolour the picture after a while but they are also very difficult to remove, if ever you should want to do so.

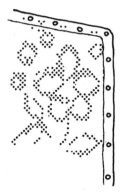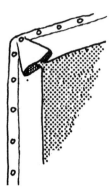

Fig. 16 Fixing materials such as tapestries over cardboard using ordinary dressmaker's pins

In cases where the work comes right to the edge of the paper, or the shape of the paper is irregular so that a rectangular cut-out mount (mat) is not possible—sometimes handmade papers are deliberately torn to leave an uneven edge, or you may have an old document with a fragment missing—pictures should be laid (mounted) directly on to the mounting board. The same techniques apply as in ordinary laying (mounting), but cut the board leaving plenty of room for trimming afterwards, and be careful not to overpaste, lest it squeezes out on to the mounting board when rolled out.

Cutting the mount or mat

General note. If you are covering the mount (mat) with bookcloth or paper, do this before you cut the window opening; linen or silk are put on afterwards as they are likely to fray.

Cut the overall size of the mount (mat) a little larger than the finished size to allow for trimming. The opening must be measured very accurately, as even a fraction of an inch can make a great difference. It should be large enough on etchings or prints to show the plate line—the raised line indicating the extent of the block from which they were printed. If there is a signature or print number these should also be visible. Otherwise the opening is measured slightly inside the picture area—about $\frac{1}{8}$" all round (figs. 17-18).

Having checked the measurements, mark the board lightly in pencil, using the non-bevelled edge of the straight edge and the set square. The blade of the knife should always be kept very sharp, as this will ensure clean edges and corners. A proper mountcutter's (mat) knife is preferable to a trimming knife as the blade can be ground thin, and it cuts through card more easily than the thicker blades of a trimming knife. Before you begin, first practice cutting bevels on spare pieces of card (cardboard) as it is harder than it looks to get a neat, professional-looking edge. Make sure the tools are clean and free from grease, as once a mount is marked it may be difficult to clean off. Place a length of spare card (cardboard) under the line to be cut to prevent marking the working surface, and on top have a piece of card (cardboard) cut as a template to work against (fig. 19). Mark this out with the straight edge as shown in fig. 20—this is lighter to work with than the heavier straight edge. Then holding the knife as shown in fig. 21 cut towards yourself with a slicing movement taking care to keep the angle of the bevel even. Tidy the corners of the bevelled edge afterwards with the tip of the knife to give a neat finish.

Covering the mounts or mats

When covering the mount (mat) with linen or silk, trim the mount to the finished size after cutting the window, then cut the material leaving a margin of about $1\frac{1}{2}$" all round the outside edge of the mount (mat). With linens, have the weave running horizontally. Paste the face side of the mount (mat) and lay this

Figs. 17-18 Measuring the watercolour for size of mount (mat) opening

Figs. 19-20 Marking out the mount (mat) before cutting

Fig. 21 Cutting the mount (mat) using a cardboard template

in the reverse side of the material. Trim the corners across. Then cut the window as in fig. 23 from the four corners to the middle, taking out the central piece but leaving a margin of approximately 1″ of material round the sight of the mount (mat). Paste the edges and turn the material over. Press well down, taking special care over the neatening of the corners.

Fig. 22 Pasting the mount (mat) before covering with linen

With silks it is not advisable to paste on the face side, owing to the delicate nature of the material. The mount (mat) can either be placed straight on to the silk, and just the inside right edges pasted, working on the outside edges before removing the window piece, or the silk can be stitched. This last method has the advantage of giving more control over the working of the silk, and prevents the weave from being pulled crooked.

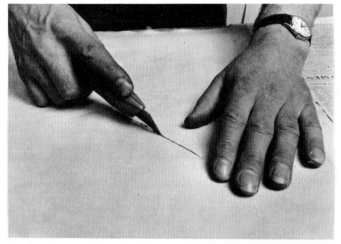

Fig. 23

Fig. 24

Fig. 25

Fig. 23 Cutting out the linen from the centre of the mount (mat) by mitring the corners

Fig. 24 Pressing down having pasted linen on reverse side of mount

Fig. 25 Pressing down the mitred corner to achieve a neat finish

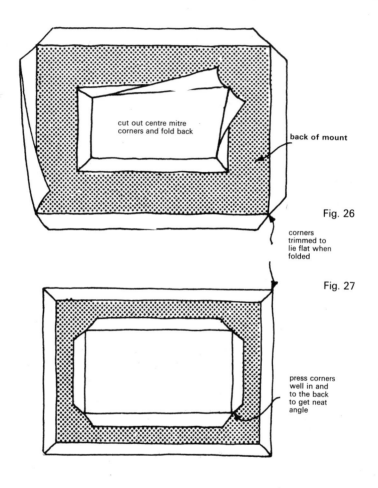

Figs. 26-27 Covering mount (mat) with linen

Fig. 28 Sewing silk mount (mat) or other fabric which cannot be pasted

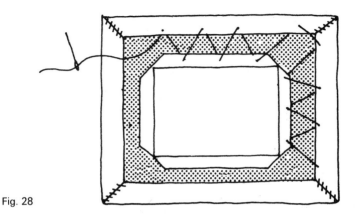

Fig. 28

Fig. 29 Map laid and framed close without a mount (mat)

Different types of mounts or mats

a *A double opening mount (mat)* is good if you have two small matching pictures which you want to put together in one frame. In fact, several small pictures can be framed together in this way.

b *A title opening.* Used if any writing to be shown is well below the edge of the picture area, or a title can be cut off and fixed to the board underneath, and the opening cut for it. This is mostly used with sporting or topographical prints.

c *A double mount (mat).* Used to give added value to the picture. The picture is either laid directly on to one board, and a separate mount cut to show $\frac{1}{4}''$ all round of the board underneath, or separate inner and outer mounts are cut — the inner one being cut first, and then the outer with a slightly larger opening.

d *A book mount (mat).* Used to show a picture if it is not to be framed. Two pieces of card (cardboard) are hinged with masking tape, with the mount (mat) cut in the upper board and the picture is hinged to the lower surface.

The addition of a gold bevel (fig. 33) can be used to effectively heighten a special work. Strips of gummed metallic gold paper are cut to a width of about $\frac{3}{8}''$, and fixed round the bevel to show about $\frac{1}{8}''$ on the face. Mitre the corners with the tip of the mounting knife (mat knife).

This paper can also be cut in lengths $\frac{1}{8}''$ wide, and these are laid about $\frac{1}{2}'' - \frac{3}{4}''$ from the window opening to form a gold line all round. Coloured lines drawn with a ruling pen and water-colour can be used with graphic works such as etchings or cartoon sketches, with addition of washlines (figs. 32-35) for a more elaborate mount (mat). Experiment with odd corners of board to see which proportions of lines and spaces suit the work best.

Fig. 30 Types of mounts (mats)

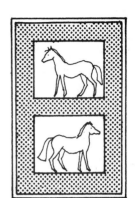

double opening mounts

a

b

c

double mount

mount with title opening

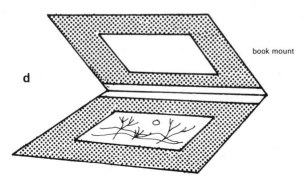

book mount

d

Fig. 31 Wooden panel set in velvet-covered mount

Fig. 32 Marking out washlines by pricking through a cardboard template to show corner marking points

Fig. 33 Bevels and use of gold paper on a mount

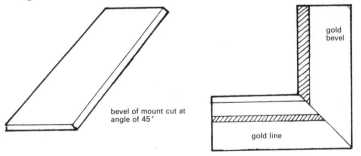

bevel of mount cut at
angle of 45°

gold
bevel

gold line

Fig. 34 Colouring in wash having previously prepared the surface with water

Fig. 35 Inking in lines with a ruling pen and watercolour

4 Joinery

Types of mouldings

Mouldings are referred to by their profile, i.e. the cross-section or end-view. Manufacturers will probably refer to each moulding by a number, and even if it has a name it may not be the same as that used by another manufacturer. However, there are a few basic shapes which may help you to describe what you want.

Choosing the moulding

Choosing the moulding may to some extent depend upon what is available. Most picture-frame moulding is only supplied whole-sale from the manufacturers, and other suppliers will only deal with personal shoppers as their range is too wide to cope with any written enquiries. This is understandable, as sending samples and dealing with small amounts could be a full-time occupation. Picture framers are usually unwilling to supply lengths of mould-ing for the same reason, and also presumably because it would not help their own trade. But many do-it-yourself shops carry stocks of picture frame mouldings, where you will probably find something to suit your purpose. Otherwise a local builder's (or lumber) yard may have mouldings that can be adapted — as these are used for building purposes there will be no rebate (rabbet) cut (fig. 36) to hold the picture, but a strip of wood at least $\frac{1}{4}$" thick can be glued or nailed on to the moulding to make a rebate (rabbet) $\frac{3}{8}$" deep. Wood from builders' merchants may tend to be rather uneven in quality and, therefore, have parts that have to be discarded, but this is offset by the fact that it will be cheaper than moulding sold specifically for picture framing.

Simple mouldings can be varied a lot in their finishes, so with a bit of imagination even the plainest wood sections can be made into decorative frames.

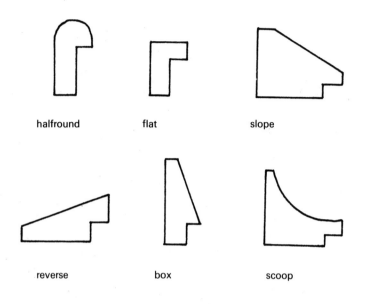

halfround   flat   slope

reverse   box   scoop

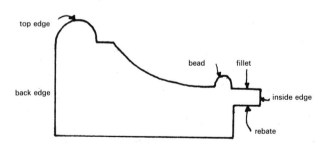

Fig. 36 Sections of mouldings

Measuring the Picture

There are two ways of measuring a picture to find the size of frame that you will need. *A rebate (rabbet) measurement* is the length that the back of the rebate will be after the mitres are cut, allowing approximately $\frac{1}{8}$" all round for insertion (fig. 37a). This is the measurement generally used for oil paintings, hardboard panels, or anything which is not easily trimmed. As some canvasses and panels may not be an exact rectangle, it is safest to measure every side and take the larger measurement to ensure that the picture will fit into the frame.

A sight measurement is the measurement from the inside edges of the front of the frame. This is used where a specific area is to be shown, such as on drawings or prints with pictures that have to be mounted (matted), the mounts (mats) can be trimmed to the correct size after the frames have been made (fig. 37b).

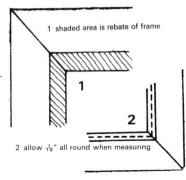

1 shaded area is rebate of frame

2 allow $\frac{1}{16}$" all round when measuring

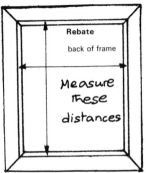

Rebate

back of frame

Measure these distances

a

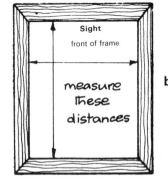

Sight

front of frame

measure these distances

b

Fig. 37

Fig. 38 Badly joined and badly fitted frame unsuitable for picture

Fig. 39 Types of simple moulding

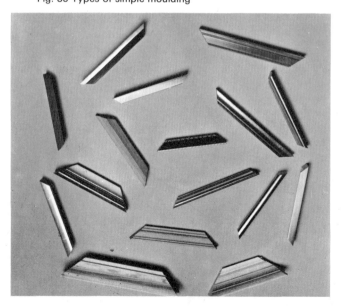

Fig. 40 Same picture correctly framed

Fig. 41 Types of complex or built-up moulding

Making the frame

Having measured the picture, mark out in pencil the four lengths needed on the moulding. Remember to add twice the width of the moulding to the actual measurements you have taken. If the length of moulding is a bit unwieldy to work with at the beginning, cut off pieces a little longer than you will actually need—these shorter lengths will be easier to control when cutting the mitres. Check all measurements carefully before cutting, as accuracy is important when dealing with fractions of an inch.

Cut the mitres from the top of the moulding to the bottom, so that any splitting of the wood will be on the inner rebate edge, and the outside corners will remain clean, and take care to keep the saw straight and vertical. The saw guides on the mitre box will keep the angle at an accurate 45°. A cutting block which can be used with a plane will help to get the mitres fitting really close after they have been sawn, and this makes all the difference to the finished appearance of the frame. Ill-fitting corners immediately draw attention to themselves (fig. 38).

Having prepared the four lengths of moulding, the frame can now be assembled. First join one long and one short side in to an L-shape in the following way. Fix one long side in the vice and coat the mitred edge with a layer of Evostik, Elmer's glue or any synthetic resin glue. Bring the mitred edge of the short side up to it, and holding the corner in position, start the holes for the nails—2 or 3 according to the width of the section (fig. 43). An electric drill is ideal if you have one, as you will only have one spare hand to work with, but otherwise a bradawl (awl) will do—preferably with a very fine head so that the wood does not split. Choose oval nails long enough to pass completely through one side of the moulding and halfway through the other. When hammering in the nails, hold the short edge slightly below the longer as the force of the hammer will then bring the joint together correctly (fig. 44). The use of both glue and nails is necessary to give a really strong joint.

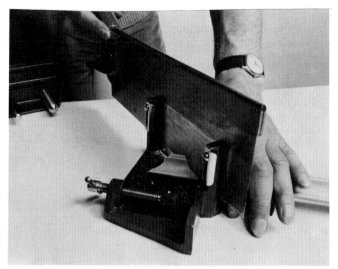

Fig. 42 Cutting moulding using a mitre-cutter

Fig. 43 Glueing the mitre before nailing

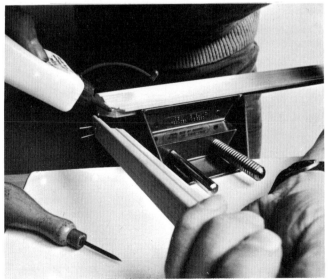

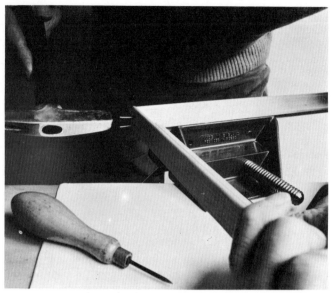

Fig. 44 Joining the frame

Drive the nails almost home, and then sink the heads to just below the surface with the nailset. Join the sides in the same manner, then complete the frame by joining these two L-shapes together always taking care to keep the corners supported. Wipe off any surplus glue and fill the nail holes with Brummer wood filling (plastic wood). This comes in various wood colours as well as in black and white, and will dry in a few minutes, after which it can be sanded down to the level of the wood.

The frame should be left to dry undisturbed for a few hours. It should either be laid flat or hung from one of its sides. But never suspend it from one of the corners as this weakens the joint.

Any faulty pieces of moulding which have to be discarded can be used for practising mitre cuts or for experimenting with different finishes. Other short pieces can be made into sample corners. These are useful for trying out different combinations if you wish to make a complex frame.

Complex frames are made up as separate frames which are finally assembled together. Start with the inner section next to the picture, and work outwards taking the measurements from the previous section. Working this out is not difficult once you have had some practice on simple frames, but the proportions of different mouldings should be taken into account. Vary the widths of the mouldings (fig. 46) as two of the same size will look unbalanced. It is better if one is wider than the others. If you use three sections, which is about the maximum recommended, the central one should be the widest. This may be either a flat panel or a slightly sloping section, and should generally be either coloured or covered in a fabric.

Inner frames or slips can be made to reduce the size of larger frames to fit smaller pictures. This, however, is only satisfactory if the picture has similar proportions to those of the frame, as the width of the slip will be the same all round, so will have the same effect of opening out the picture as a wide mount.

5 Covering panels

If you are making a wide frame that has a centre member, this panel may be covered with fabric. Prepared mouldings can be bought with linen already fixed, but these are not normally available (fig. 2). Suitable types of materials are listed in chapter 2 and you should try to keep a few samples of linens and velvets, as they are useful to try out against the picture when choosing the fabric. Remember that the texture of the material must be taken into account as well as the colour: velvet and coarse linen are suitable for strong oil paintings, fine linen or bookcloth for more delicate pictures. Useful colours are soft greys, olive greens, and light browns. Bright coloured velvets are decorative as a background for displaying small objects such as medals or low relief carvings and the same material can also be used on the slip or panel to make a showcase effect.

The centre member should be covered before the frame is finally assembled. Since the edges of this section will be covered by the rebates (rabbets) of the outer and inner sections of the frame, the fabric can be cut to the exact width of the member and the edges left as they are (fig. 45).

Using a very sharp knife to get a clean edge and cut four strips of material; each should measure a little longer than the actual length of each side of the frame as the corners will be mitred and trimmed later (fig. 45a). Stick down the material working round the frame. The paste should be used sparingly otherwise it will come through and mark the fabric. Take special care with the edges and make sure that they are well stuck down. If insufficient paste is used, little blisters may later appear which cannot be removed once the paste has dried. Cut the mitres on the corners,

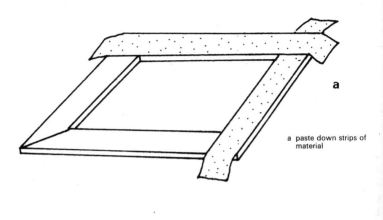

a

a paste down strips of
material

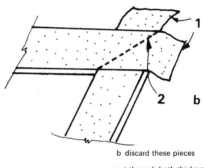

1

2

b

b discard these pieces

cut through both thicknesses
of material

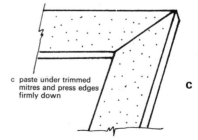

c paste under trimmed
mitres and press edges
firmly down

c

Fig. 45 Covering a panel
with fabric

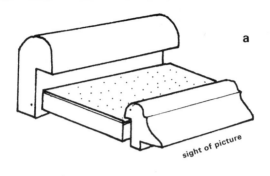

a

sight of picture

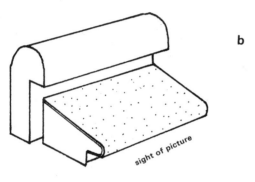

b

sight of picture

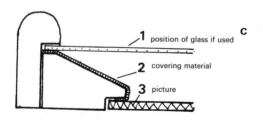

c

1 position of glass if used

2 covering material

3 picture

which should correspond exactly to the mitres on the frame. Cut through the double thickness of the material on the corners so that the edges fit closely together (fig. 45b). A small steel edge and a sharp razor blade will enable you to get a clean, straight line. Finally paste under the trimmed mitres (fig. 45c).

If you are covering an inner frame or slip (insert) that will be next to the picture, the raw edge of the material will have to be turned under, and therefore the width of the material must be cut wide enough to allow for this (fig. 46b). Work in the same way as before, but take special care with the inner edge to make sure that the material is stuck smoothly round it. The mitres should be cut very carefully by hand on the inner edge, again using a razor blade and working slowly. You will find that it takes a little practice to achieve a really neat corner.

If glass is to be used, this should be fitted between the centre member and the outer frame to protect the fabric (fig. 46c).

Fig. 46 Fitting a fabric covered panel

6 Finishing

Once the frame has been made it must be 'finished' before the picture is finally fitted into it. Prepared mouldings, of course, need no finishing, but all plain wood mouldings have to be treated in some way. If the wood is of a sufficiently good quality with a pleasant grain, the frame can be left as natural wood and finished with a wax polish. Otherwise the moulding can be coloured. With imagination a variety of finishes can be obtained with just a few materials, and the same moulding can be treated in many different ways. Before you start work on the frame itself, experiment with off-cuts of the actual moulding you have used and this will give you an idea of how the picture will look in the finished frame. Take into account where the picture is going to hang so that the overall effect will be in keeping with the surroundings. It is difficult to give precise rules for colouring, for, as mentioned earlier, this depends on personal taste and different people's interpretations can produce a variety of results, but to start with a few basic rules may help.

A single moulding framing a watercolour or print will look best if left as plain waxed wood, or finished in a light neutral colour (fig. 47). A delicate picture, such as a fine drawing, should never be put in too dark a frame as the eye is immediately drawn to the frame rather than to the picture. A darker finish can be used for a bold picture in black and white or where the colours are strong. Black should only be used on mouldings up to $\frac{3}{4}''$ wide, and then with discretion. Very brightly coloured frames are best avoided.

Fig. 47 F. Toledo *The Jump* 1965. Gouache fixed on thin plywood and laid (mounted) on linen to form a panel, with natural wood frame

Fig. 48 Alfred Daniels *Bankside*. Gouache painting with linen mount (mat) and prepared silver moulding

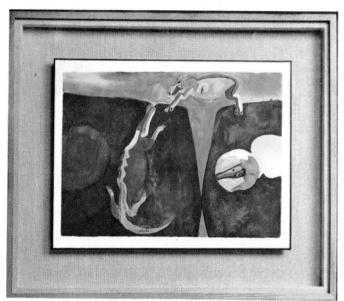

47

48

Fig. 49 Picture and decorated mount by John Eric Brown in coloured inks with simple gilt frame.

White frames tend to drain a picture of colour, particularly where pastel shades are concerned. Note that the colour of the mount (if you have one) should always be taken into account as well as the colours in the picture.

The same general rules apply to oil paintings with additional considerations for complex frames. Where a complex frame is used, the inner section should act as a visual link between the picture and the frame and, therefore, a light neutral shade is often the answer. You will find that pure white will probably be too strong a contrast, unless it is broken with a little colour. The relationship between the other sections must always be borne in mind if the result is to be successful and the whole effect should be kept simple both in colour and texture.

With light paintings a darker overall effect for the frame is often the most pleasing. On the other hand, the same treatment against a dark painting would be too sombre altogether, so keep the tone of the frame light. The moulding can be tinted either to pick up, or to contrast with, the colours in the picture—for instance, the frame of a landscape made-up predominantly of greens could be coloured greeny-grey.

When working on a complex frame you will find it easier to work on each section separately. (Remember that if linen, or velvet, is to be used on the centre panels this should be fixed into position before the frame is finally assembled.)

Natural wood finish

If the wood is to be left plain and waxed, first make sure that there are no imperfections in the wood which will show up. Any cracks in the mitred corners and any nail holes (if you haven't filled them already) should be filled with wood filling (plastic wood). The frame can then be sanded down with grade 1 sandpaper to give a smooth finish, and then polished with white wax polish (ordinary household or beeswax) and a soft cloth.

Staining

Stains are available in a variety of colours including dark oak, red brown and silver grey. As they bring out the grain of the wood, as opposed to the gesso and paint method of colouring which conceals it, be sure that the wood is of sufficiently good quality to stand this treatment. If the stains are used undiluted they will produce a very intense colour, so they are generally diluted with methylated spirit (alcohol) to the required weakness. They should be applied with a brush, and when dry the frame can be lightly rubbed down and wax polished.

Gesso

If the frames are to be painted, the wood must be coated with gesso first. This may sound an elaborate process, but it provides a necessary base for the paint which would otherwise sink straight into the wood. Gesso is a white powder akin to plaster-of-Paris, and is the basic preparation for all gilded and colour work. To make up the preparation for use, the gesso is mixed with rabbit-skin size which is obtained in sheet form. The size is soaked in cold water for not more than eight hours until it is rubbery. One sheet of size is melted in one and a half pints of water. This should not be allowed to boil. Gesso powder is added to the size solution, stirring continuously, until the consistency is that of milk. A little

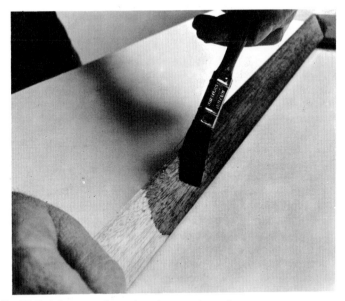
Fig. 50 Staining natural wood to show up the grain

is tested on the new frame and it should be almost opaque when it is ready for use. The gesso solution should be kept in a water-bath until used. When cold it solidifies and if heated over a flame will burn and form into lumps unless a water-bath is used. For colour work two coats of gesso are used to give a resilient finish. The gesso should be brushed on to the frame, left to dry, and then given a second coat. When this is dry the surface can be lightly rubbed down and will then be ready for colouring.

Colouring

A good finish can be obtained by mixing acryllic paint with white or black emulsion paint. These are easy to work, and produce a quick drying waterproof surface which can later be wax-polished.

Acryllic paints can be bought in small tubes quite inexpensively, and with the basic earth colours, umbers, sienas and ocres, and the primary colours, a range of subtle neutral shades can be obtained. Enough colour should be well mixed with a little water to allow for 2 or 3 coats, as it is difficult to repeat the colour exactly. Try it on a piece of the moulding before starting work. Brush the paint on fairly quickly to get an even finish, taking care not to flood the corners.

Colour can also be stippled on afterwards with cotton wool to create a marbled effect, or to break up the flat surface of the paint. Rounded moulding can be coloured to simulate bamboo in this way.

It is not advisable to use gold and silver paints to colour frames. The colour generally has a crude appearance if applied to large areas. If a metallic finish is required it is preferable to use prepared mouldings. Pelikan gold and silver water paints can be used with discretion, perhaps to colour an inner fillet or the bead of a frame.

Gilding See chapter 8.

7 Fitting

Fitting is the process of fixing the picture into the frame. Oil paintings, paintings on hardboard, wooden panels and anything not requiring glass or other backing, can be fixed in position simply with panel pins (brads) (figs. 53-55). The nails must not, of course, be driven through the actual work, or hammered in so hard that they penetrate the face of the frame. With a complex frame the members should be nailed together starting with the inner section and working outwards.

Glass

Unless you are doing a large amount of framing, it is simpler to have the glass cut to the size you need at a local glass merchants (glazier). Picture glass is thinner and clearer than window glass, without the flaws, and is known as 18 oz. glass. Non-reflecting glass is obtainable, but is considerably more expensive and tends to dull the colours of the picture. If you are cutting glass, use the cutter recommended and work on a surface which will not mark the glass. Latex is ideal but an old blanket will do. Never run the cutter over the same cut more than once, as this only tends to shatter the glass but also ruins the cutting point (fig. 51).

Hardboard backing

This can also be bought cut to size at a lumber yard or do-it-yourself shop, but it may be more economical to buy large sheets and cut it yourself. Use the glass as a template, mark round it in pencil on the hardboard and then cut it to the required size, trimming with a knife.

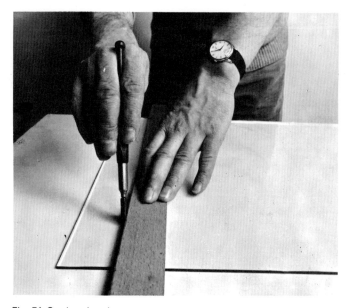

Fig. 51 Cutting the glass

Assembling the frame

Everything should be clean and free from dust. The glass can be given a final light polish with methylated spirit (alcohol), and the picture and mount should be checked for any marks. If the trimming of the mount has been left till now, the glass can again be used as a template to mark it to the correct size, using a ruler to

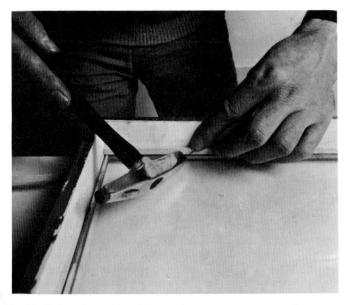

Fig. 52 Fixing glass with a fillet, as for pastels, to prevent the picture touching the glass

get the margins even. Fit everything together, and nail lightly into the frame from the back, using $\frac{3}{4}''$ panel pins (brads) (fig. 56). The use of a fitting block held against the frame while nailing will give a more rigid surface, particularly if the moulding is narrow. A fitting block is simply a small block of wood covered in felt or baize (fig. 58). Finally seal round the back of the frame with strips of gummed brown paper tape as a protection against dust (fig. 57).

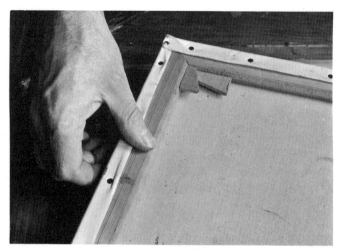

Fig. 53

Fig. 54

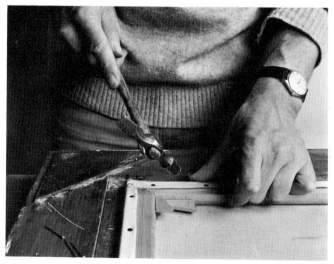

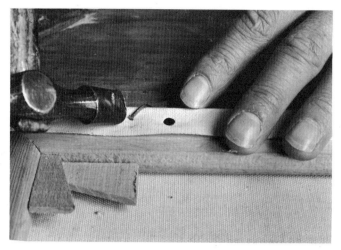

Fig. 55

Figs. 53-55 Fitting a canvas into a frame

Pastels should be separated from the glass by a thin strip of wood concealed between the glass and the picture, otherwise the surface may rub off on to the glass (fig. 52). Similarly, when the backboard is hammered into the frame very carefully it should be done so that the movement does not dislodge particles of the medium.

If the back of the picture is required to be seen in addition to

Fig. 56

the front, as in the case of a document or letter, the hardboard backing can be replaced by another sheet of glass. This can be secured by a fillet of wood, but the moulding used for the frame must have a sufficient rebate (rabbet) to allow for the extra thickness and weight.

Spring clips (fig. 59) can be used for fitting oils if the picture is to be easily removable. Turn screws are used for the same purpose on pictures with glass, such as mounted work, so that the work can be slipped out without difficulty when required.

Fig. 57

Fig. 56 Fitting a picture with hardboard backing

Fig. 57 Stripping the back of the frame with gummed brown paper

Fig. 58 Fitting a picture with a narrow moulding using a fitting block to keep the work rigid

Fig. 59 Methods of hanging pictures

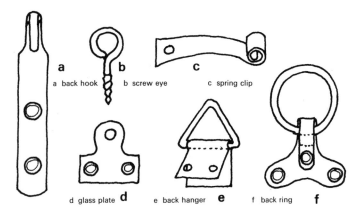

a back hook   b screw eye   c spring clip

d glass plate   e back hanger   f back ring

Methods of hanging pictures

Having framed the picture, the final step is to hang it correctly. The first thing to check is that the fixtures used are sufficiently strong to carry the weight of the picture. There are various types that can be used.

Backhangers (fig. 59e). These are used on small, light frames where the moulding is too narrow to have anything screwed into it. These are fitted into the backboard before the frame is assembled. Two slits are cut with the trimming (x-actor) knife about 2″ down from the top and in 2″ from the side of the backboard. The hangers are then pushed through and the two flanges hammered flat on the inside of the backboard. The wire is twisted between the hangers.

Screw eyes (fig. 59b). These can be used if the moulding is wide enough to take screws without splitting the wood, and is the simplest form of hanging. Equal distances should be marked approximately a third of the way down from the top of the frame with a ruler and small holes made with a bradawl (awl) to make screwing easier (fig. 49). The wire should be twisted between the screw eyes, fairly tightly so that when the picture is hung the wire will not show above the top edge of the frame.

Back rings and back hooks (fig. 59a/f). These are used on wide mouldings when the picture is heavy. The position of the fittings should be marked as for screw eyes. Wire is again fixed between them.

Glass plates (fig. 59d). These are generally used for mirrors and for permanent fixing to the wall. They can be screwed to any section of the upper part of the moulding so that the hole for screwing into the wall protrudes beyond the edge of the moulding. When fixing to the wall make sure that the screws are sufficiently long to ensure a really safe fitting.

Picture wire for hanging can be obtained from most good hardware shops, but do make sure that you have wire of the correct strength. Never use string, even as a temporary measure,

Fig. 60 Marking positions for hanging

as it will eventually fray and break, and you may forget to replace it before the picture has fallen off the wall.

Avoid hanging the picture too high where it cannot be seen; approximately at eye level is probably the best general position, but you can judge this best by trying the picture in different places before deciding where to put the picture hooks. These special hooks usually come in about three sizes and can be obtained from most good hardware shops. There is a single hook, fixed to the wall by a nail driven through it, which will bear the weight of light pictures. A double hook is better for heavier pictures and for a very heavy picture, two double hooks placed a little way in from the edges of the moulding will help to balance the picture more evenly.

8 Gilding

As explained in the introduction, gilding is a specialised craft, but for those who may be particularly interested in this process I include this chapter.

A frame must be carefully prepared prior to gilding. The materials used are as follows:

Gesso

For gold work, two coats of hard gesso (preparation as described on p. 70), and two coats of Number 2, a softer gesso, are used. Number 2 is prepared by adding more gesso powder to the existing mixture. As it contains more gesso, it has a greater covering power. Over the Number 2 are laid four coats of Soft White which is made with gelatine or parchment size, and which is a much heavier and softer gesso mixture. The purpose of the Soft White is to obtain a burnish. Each coat is applied as the previous one is drying to avoid air bubbles and flaking-off.

English red

This is a clay which when bought wet, resembles modelling clay. A knob of clay is added to liquid gelatine or parchment size, until the mixture is smooth and cream-like so that when warm it drops from a brush in a stream.

French red

This is bought in cones, and needs to be soaked before use. The water is strained off when ready and the clay beaten to a pulp. Preparation is the same as for English clay.

Gold

Gold is obtained in looseleaf form for water-gilding or transfer form for oil-gilding. Water-gilding will be described here.

Tools

1 A cush, which is a chamois leather pad.
2 A gilding knife.
3 Several different-sized tips. A tip is a flat, fine brush, usually of squirrel hair, used for picking up the gold.
4 Several burnishers. A burnisher is a specially polished smooth, hard stone mounted on a handle.
5 Several soft brushes.
6 A small pot of water containing a small amount of melted gelatine and a little methylated spirit (alcohol).

Fig. 61 Picking up gold leaf with the knife

When the preparation has been made up, the gesso is applied vigorously to the frame to work into the grain of the wood. After two coats have been applied the surface is rubbed down with fine sandpaper. All gesso dust must be removed before the Number 2 is applied. This fills in the risen grain. The surface is again rubbed down before four coats of Soft White are applied. This forms a smooth surface for the gold, after rubbing down with the finest grade sandpaper.

The first coat of clay is thinly applied with a mop brush, working away from the mitres. The second coat is applied only when the first is completely dry. Four coats are applied altogether for bright gold work. When completely dry, the surface is then smoothed with very fine grade wet and dry emery paper and cleaned with spirit (alcohol) to free from grease and dust, and polished with tissue. The surface is now ready to start gilding.

A mop brush is dipped into the water/gelatine solution and the clay surface given an even coat of water, making it tacky. Gold leaf is applied to the frame with the tip. A few sheets of gold are emptied on to the cush. It will need *gentle* blowing to smooth the leaves (fig. 62). The gold can be arranged with the knife and cut to a suitable size (fig. 63). The tip is brushed on the face (hair) to pick up a slight amount of grease from the skin (fig. 64). This should be enough to enable a piece of gold to be picked up on the tip. Brush the surface of the clay with water (fig. 65). The gold is then gently applied to the slightly wet clay. It is most important that excess water is removed as it can seep through holes in the gold. The pieces of gold should be overlapped as little as possible. The small bubbles which appear after laying the gold can be removed by gently tapping with a soft brush (fig. 66).

When the frame has been covered with gold, it is left to dry. To test if it is dry, the surface is tapped with a burnisher. If a dull sound is produced, the frame is still too wet. If a light ring is produced, the frame is dry enough to work on further.

Burnishing is the process which gives the bright appearance to the surface. The burnisher is applied to the frame in long even

Fig. 62 Gold ready for cutting

Fig. 63 Cutting the gold leaf

Fig. 64 Greasing the brush before picking up the gold

Fig. 65 Brushing the red clay with water before laying the gold

strokes, using light hand pressure only. This is very delicate work: hard pressure causes pitting of the surface and the gold scratches easily.

It will be found that after the frame is burnished, small areas of gold will not have adhered to the surface. The frame is 'faulted' by applying small pieces of gold in the same manner as described, except that clean water which does not contain gelatine should be used. This is to prevent build-up of size.

Simple antiqued and colour work

Less preparation is required, as it is the preparation which gives the degree of brightness to the gold on the frame and a high burnish is not required on antiqued work. It is unnecessary to fault an antiqued frame, and a dullish, warm tone to the gold is given by gentle application of substances such as pigmented wax (e.g. shoe polish) and diluted spirit (alcohol) or water stains.

Fig. 66 Fixing the gold with a dry brush

Fig. 67 Small pastel portrait by Daniel Caffe in gold leaf frame with linen slip (insert)

Fig. 68 Fabric collage in old maple frame

Fig. 69 Saito *Hokkaido*. Woodcut with no mount (mat), wood slope and prepared silver moulding

Fig. 67

Fig. 68

Fig. 69

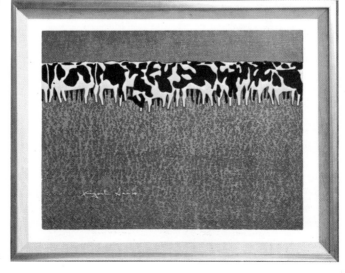

9 Box frames

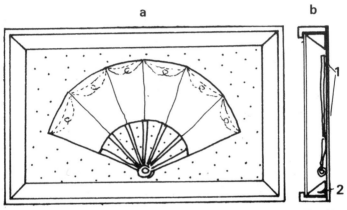

a

b

1 fan fixed on to backboard by
wiring through from the back
in several places
2 slope wide enough to hold
glass well clear of fan

Fig. 70 A box frame

Box frames are needed when anything three-dimensional is being
framed. As mentioned earlier, there are unlimited possibilities in
the objects that can be framed, ranging from a fabric collage,
which may only require a shallow box, to low relief carvings
needing a box of greater depth. The usual composition of a box
frame is a backboard to which the object is fixed, a slope deep
enough to stand clear of it, and an outer moulding. Glass is fixed
between the slope and the outer moulding. (Fig. 70.)

A fabric collage can be laid (mounted) directly on to the backboard (and this would determine the size of the frame) but in the case of smaller objects, the backboard is cut to give a reasonably wide margin all round the object, so that it does not look cramped. Cotton velvets look very effective in this type of frame as the rich colours make an excellent background which shows objects off to their best advantage. Linens and bookcloths are also suitable, but synthetic fabrics should be avoided as they are difficult to stick down and liable to fray. If a fabric covering is used, the backboard should first be cut to the correct size and then covered with the chosen fabric before the object is fixed.

Methods of fixing will naturally vary depending on the object. Those such as cameos, medals, medallions, miniatures and fans can usually be attached invisibly by fine wire from the back. Tiny holes are bored through the backboard and wire inserted from the back to loop through a ring or anything which will hold. The wire is then drawn through to the back of the board and twisted round. Anything with a wooden or card paper back can simply be stuck with a strong glue such as Evostik (or Elmer's glue). Remember that the objects will eventually be hanging vertically, so be sure that they are secure.

The slope can also be covered in the same fabric as the background by the method described in chapter 5. This will give a showcase effect to the frame, but you may prefer to have a natural wood finish as described in the chapter on finishing.

The frame is finally assembled in the normal way, though in this case the glass should be cut to fit the outer moulding and not the backboard.

10 Using old frames

Occasionally it is possible to make use of second-hand frames and old frames as long as they are not in too bad a condition. If they are in very good condition, they will often only need refitting with new glass and backboard. If they are in very bad condition, they are best discarded.

Carved wood frames and plaster or composition frames

Genuine carved wood frames are rare and valuable and should only be restored by experts. What are often mistakenly referred to as carved wood frames are in fact plaster mouldings laid (mounted) upon a wooden base. With age the plaster tends to chip and crumble and it is unsatisfactory to repair. If the moulding is in good condition, it is very simple to recolour it after a preliminary surface cleaning with a damp sponge. Avoid gold and silver paint, even if the temptation is great, as this produces a very garish effect. If, however, the plaster is in bad condition it can be removed to reveal the wood underneath. This will usually be a fairly plain frame, but it can sometimes have an attractive section. Removing plaster is a messy job and should be undertaken outside if possible. The frame should be laid flat and covered with wet rags and sawdust and left to soak thoroughly for a few days. After this time the plaster will scrape off easily.

Maple frames

Maple frames have become fashionable in recent years so that the price has increased considerably. The warm colour of the wood

Fig. 71 A plaster frame and a linen slip (insert) with a gold bevel

is very pleasing and will look good against a variety of different pictures (fig. 68). If care is taken with the veneered finish these frames can be cut down satisfactorily to fit a smaller picture.

Fig. 72 Eighteenth-century corner pattern carved frame

List of suppliers

The local classified telephone directory will give you names of builders' merchants (lumber yards) and also do-it-yourself shops (and glaziers) who will supply some mouldings and hardboard, and tell you where to get glass cut if they do not stock it themselves.

ENGLAND

Mouldings
J. Bebb Ltd, 169 Hackney Road, London E2

Adhesives
Associated Adhesives (resins and glue and paste). Hardware shops and stationers.

Tools
Buck and Ryan Ltd, 101 Tottenham Court Road, London W1. Branches all over the country.

Gilding materials
George M. Whiley Ltd, 54 Whitfield Street, London W1

Mounting boards and papers
Clifford Milburn and Co., 54 Fleet Street, London EC4. Paper by the sheet for covering mounting boards, including hand-made papers.
T. N. Lawrence and Sons, 2 Bleeding Heart Lane, Grenville Street, London EC1

Materials for covering boards and panels
Winterbottom Products, bookcloth, 27 Chancery Lane, London WC1
B. Barnet and Co. Ltd, 22 Garrick Street, London WC2

Hanging materials
(Hook-it adjustable wire corners for use with glass and back-board for hanging unframed pictures.)
A. V. Pilley, 7 Hill Road, London NW8

UNITED STATES

Adhesives
Casein glue (Elmers-Weldwood) source: hardware store, paint store.
Synthetic Latex (Atex No. 16)
Casein base (Pictex No. 17) source: **Adhesive Products**, Inc, 1660 Bronx, New York

Tools
Mitre-box (Stanley No. 150)
Corner clamp (Stanley No. 404) source: hardware store or **Stanley Tools**, New Britain, Conn.
Gilder's tip, source: paint store, sign painter's supply store
Roller, source: art store, printer's supply store
Other tools, source: hardware store, paint store, art store

Paints
Vinyl base or latex base, source: paint store **(Lucite, Pronto, Super, Kemstone, etc.)**

Gilding materials
Gold leaf and metal leaf, source: paint store, art store, sign painter's supply store

Mat boards and papers,
source: art store

Materials for covering boards and panels
Linen, source: **Utrect Linens**, 119 W. 57 Street, New York 19, art store.

For further reading

The Art and History of Frames by Henry Heydenrick. Vane, London, 1964

Picture Framing by Max Hyder. Pitman, New York, 1963

Picture Framing by Edward Landon. New York Artist's Group, New York, 1945

Index